Henry W. Howgate

Polar Colonization and Exploration

Henry W. Howgate

Polar Colonization and Exploration

ISBN/EAN: 9783337162009

Printed in Europe, USA, Canada, Australia, Japan

Cover: Foto ©ninafisch / pixelio.de

More available books at www.hansebooks.com

POLAR COLONIZATION

AND

EXPLORATION.

NORTH POLAR REGIONS
OF THE
WESTERN HEMISPHERE

G R A N

farthest point

C. Britannia Sighted by Beaumont

Beaumont's farthest North.
Mt Farragut

POLAR COLONIZATION.

To the Honorable Senators and Members of the forty-fourth Congress this brief memoir is respectfully submitted, in the hope that its perusal will convince them of the wisdom of supporting the plan for establishing a temporary Arctic colony which it sets forth, and in the hope that, under the direction of Divine Providence, it may prove of service in promoting and furthering the attainment of an object so worthy alike of national ambition and of national success.

HENRY W. HOWGATE.

ARCTIC EXPLORATION.

In the House of Represenatives, January 8, 1877. Read twice, referred to the Committee on Naval Affairs, and ordered to be printed.

Mr. Hunter, on leave, introduced the following bill : A bill to authorize and equip an expedition to the Arctic Seas.

"*Be it enacted by the Senate and House of Representatives of the United States of America in Congress assembled*, That the President of the United States be authorized to organize and send out one or more expeditions toward the north pole, and to establish a temporary colony, for purposes of exploration, at some point north of the eighty-first degree of north latitude, on or near the shore of Lady Franklin Bay ; to detail such officers or other persons of the public service to take part in the same as may be necessary, and to use any public vessel that may be suitable for the purpose ; the scientific operations of the expedition to be prosecuted in accordance with the advice of the National Academy of Science ; and that the sum of fifty thousand dollars, or such part therof as may be necessary, be hereby appropriated out of any moneys in the Treasury not otherwise appropriated, to be expended under the direction of the President: *Provided*, that no part of the sum so appropriated shall be carried to the surplus fund or covered into the Treasury until the purpose of the appropriation shall have been completed, but may be applied to expenses of said expedition incurred during any subsequent year that said expedition may be engaged in its duties."

INTRODUCTORY.

The history of Arctic exploration is one of the most thrilling interest, and its pages, whether turned by the hands of youth or of maturer years, enchain alike the faculties of thought and fancy with a weird fascination akin to that whereby the "ancient mariner" held the wedding guest a captive to his will. Since the days of the gallant Frobisher—the first Englishman who sailed in search of the famous northwest passage—of Raleigh, Drake and Hawkins, the gallant men of Devon, and of the fated Hendrick Hudson, who perished so miserably upon his ill-starred quest, down to the latter times of Ross and Parry, of the canonized Franklin and the unfortunate Hall, the icy barriers of the Pole have guarded, still unsolved, their strange, mysterious riddle, as surely as the Egyptian sphinx has kept its hidden lore beneath the burning sands of an equally inhospitable clime. The lists of holy martyrdom contain no names illuminated by a purer piety, the rolls of chivalry no titles gilded by deeds of greater prowess, than the history of that strange region has given to an admiring world or shrouded from the knowledge of mankind behind its unlifted veil of mystery. Men of many diverse nations have penetrated those gloomy fastnesses to wage fierce warfare for the sake of science and of gain, while the impelling motives of the navigators have been as various as their nationalities. The love of adventure which stimulated the hardy sons of Devon was spurred to more earnest action by visions of Cathay, but the lust for gold which sought its outlet and highway in the "northwest passage" has not alone inspired the breasts of those who made the oft-recurring journeys over this frozen road to honor. The high minded sentiments of honorable governments who would not leave to unknown fates the gallant sons whom they sent forth to conquer nature, and the undying love of a great lady for her missing lord—a love which knew no shadow of change through time or doubt or distance—these nobler causes have contributed more than all else to emblazon the pages of Arctic history with names whose lustre time can never dim. Nor has mankind alone been the explorer of these hidden regions. Ships manned by no human hands have sailed the ice bound seas. Steered by the helmsman Fate upon their unknown voyage through Boreal solitudes they have yet returned staunch, taut and seaworthy; and although no human intelligence traced upon the log book any record of the cruise, still they have told to practical eyes truths which have aided the unraveling of the great primeval mystery.

The history of several abandonded whaling vessels, and more particularly of the *Resolute*—her fifteen months' solitary cruise and subsequent recovery—is too well known to need further mention here.

But the glamor of romance and the intense longing to grapple with and solve the mysteries of the unknown—strong though their influence may be upon the human mind and the human inclination—sink to utter insignificance when compared with the nobler aims which urge mankind toward the conquest of the Pole. Almost every department, of terrestrial and celestial science alike, abounds with great problems whose solution will be found alone behind the icy barriers of the North, and to a few of these the attention of the reader will be briefly directed.

GEOGRAPHY.

This science will derive most substantial benefits and additions from further Polar research. To ascertain whether the Polar sea contains important lands or islands scattered throughout it, and to settle finally the true configuration of Greenland, may be noted as two of the most important points to be decided.

HYDROGRAPHY AND METEOROLOGY.

Already in these two great branches of science, so important, not only to the needs of trade and commerce, but to our daily wants and existence, the United States are in advance of all the nations of the earth, and in no other region are discoveries so important to be looked for as will doubtless be made within the Polar basin. The question of ocean streams and currents, where the Gulf stream and Kurosiwo end and the Polar current commences, with the phenomena attending the diurnal rise and fall of the tides, the direction, changes, velocity and character of winds, also many questions of temperature, can nowhere be studied with absolute success unless it be within this wondrous area.

GEODESY.

A series of observations upon the vibrations of a pendulum swinging in the immediate vicinity of the Pole can alone accurately determine the true configuration of the earth and settle definitely many disputed points connected with the laws of gravity which are still uncertain. Upon these important subjects some of the most valuable information yet obtained has been gained from the careful and thorough experiments made by the scientific members of the *Polaris* expedition, experiments under the direction of our own National Academy of Science.

MAGNETISM, ASTRONOMY, &C.

Terrestrial magnetism and atmospheric electricity can be studied in these regions more satisfactorily and with better prospects of important discovery than in any other portion of the globe. In solar and stellar chemistry, numberless facts concerning the solar corona and the zodiacal and auroral lights are yet wanting to a more perfect knowledge of the science and its laws, facts which must be looked for near the Pole, and there alone. The study of the spectrum of the sun, the aurora, and the Arctic twilight, will yield rich and increasing treasurers of knowledge. A phenomena defying all description and accurate classification, its study in high latitudes by careful observers, and the spectrum analysis will yield new and important truths to science. The Arctic winter is a more pleasant season for such observations than is usually supposed. The long Polar night is said to be "more endurable and more enjoyable" with its corruscating splendors of the aurora borealis, than the same season further south, with its mist and fog. To quote Dr. Kane, "the intense beauty of the Arctic firmament can hardly be imagined; it looked close above our heads, with its stars magnified in glory, and the very planets twinkling so much as to baffle the observation of our astronomer."

MINERALOGY.

The Polar regions are rich in this department. Graphite, and other useful minerals are abundant, while cryolite, the double fluoride of sodium and aluminum, which has been found so invaluable in the industrial arts of this country, is not known to exist in any other part of the world. Gold has also been found, and a colony remaining for several seasons would probably be able to determine the extent and value of the auriferous deposits.

GEOLOGY, ETHNOLOGY, ETC.

The geology of this distant clime is especially worthy of

close and extended study, while its flora and fauna are of the greatest interest to the naturalist. The Arctic regions are the richest of the world in fossil remains, and in the department of Ethnology suggest an inquiry of equal interest and importance. In latitude 81° 30′, Captain Hall found traces of human beings, and if land should be found at the pole, within the Polar sea, traces may be discovered of that race of Arctic Highlanders, anterior to the Esquimaux, of whose former existence Sir John Ross obtained such indubitable proofs.*

It is impossible in a brief memoir to do more than glance, in the briefest manner, at the principal triumphs which are to be won in these far distant regions and in the cause of science, while the absolute poverty of any summary, so attempted, can readily be imagined when it is remembered that the volume of scientific instruction and suggestion, prepared under the direction of the British Royal Society, or the guidance of Arctic explorers, contained nearly 800 pages.

From the year 860, when Naddodr, the Norwegian, sailed northwest toward the Arctic regions and discovered the island of Iceland, down to the departure of Captain Allen Young from England, in 1876, to communicate with the depots of the *Alert* and the *Discovery* under Captain Nares, there have been no less than two hundred Arctic voyages of which we possess authentic record. In the 9th century there was one, in the tenth one, in the eleventh, twelfth, thirteenth and fourteenth centuries, one each. Then they commence to increase very rapidly in numbers, for in the fifteenth century there were three; in the sixteenth, twenty-two, and in the seventeenth, thirty-eight; while from 1800 to 1850 there were thirty-seven, and from 1851 to 1876, no less than sixty-nine expeditions.

It is only necessary here, however, to glance rapidly at five of the most recent Arctic voyages.

DE HAVEN'S EXPEDITION.

This was first in order of those which may be considered purely American, and was fitted out by the United States Government, but chiefly at the cost of Mr. Henry Grinnell,

---

* There prevails, indeed, even now, among the Esquimaux, traditions of lands far north of their own, inhabited by a people superior to themselves in knowledge and intelligence; lands where long bearded men fatten the musk ox and where churches and clocks are found.

of New York City. It consisted of two small brigs, the
Advance, of 140, and the *Rescue*, of 90 tons; was organized
for the purpose of exploration, and also of searching for the
missing Sir John Franklin, being designed to co-operate
with several English expeditions for the same purpose which
had started for, or were already cruising within the Arctic
circle. The expedition was commanded with distinguished
ability and zeal throughout by Lieutenant Edwin J. DeHaven, of the United States Navy, and sailed from New York
May 24, 1850, accompanied, as surgeon and naturalist, by
the celebrated Eastern and Arctic explorer, Dr. Kane, of
whom more hereafter. The plan of the expedition was to
push forward, without delay, toward Bank's Land and Melville Island, and generally to make the best use of every
opportunity for exploring in that direction. At this time
there were within the Eastern Arctic waters no less than
eleven vessels belonging to various exploring expeditions.
DeHaven visited Cape Riley and Beechy Island, about three
miles west of the cape and just at the entrance of Wellington Channel, in the latter part of August, where traces of
the Franklin party had been found, and wintered in the vicinity of ships of the other expeditions. The spring of
1851 was devoted to land explorations, in which the shores
of Wellington Channel, the coast of Bank's Land, and the
waters leading from Barrow's Strait to Melville Island, were
thoroughly explored. DeHaven, with his compeers, dicov-
ered 675 miles of hitherto unknown coast, and to him and
his expedition belongs exclusively the honor of discovering
Grinnell Land, to the north and west of Smith's Sound and
Kennedy Channel. Finally, their expedition, which had
gallantly led the way wherever they could go, and whose
commander carned for himself at the hands of the English
the sobriquet of " the mad Yankee," after enduring much
suffering and danger, arrived in New York, the *Advance* on
September 30, and the *Rescue* on October 3, 1851, having
been absent a little over sixteen months, and having wintered within the Arctic seas. It is worthy of notice here
that Lieutenant DeHaven invariably found that the water of
the Polar seas preserved beneath the ice a temperature of
28° Fahrenheit, or 4° below the melting point of fresh
water ice.

DR. KANE'S EXPEDITION.

This expedition was another of those sent out in search of

Sir John Franklin. It was fitted out at the expense of the United States, Mr. Grinnell and Mr. George Peabody; sailed from New York May 30, 1853, and followed the Smith Sound route. Kane wintered in 1853-54 in Rensselaer Bay, on the western coast of Greenland in latitude 78° 37' north. Leaving his ship, the *Advance*, he made a boat journey to Upernavik, 6° further south, and next traced Kennedy Channel, the northerly prolongation of Smith's Sound, to latitude 81° 22' north, and sighted the highest northerly land which had been seen up to that time. Hayes, who accompanied him, reached a still higher latitude in dog-sledges. Members of the expedition saw an open sea to the north of Kennedy Channel with tides which ebbed and flowed, and these tides must have come from the Atlantic ocean, most probably by and through the North Atlantic Channel. Members of this expedition, during its stay in these regions, penetrated as far as latitude 80° 35', a point named by them Cape Constitution, in Washington Land. On May 17, 1855, they abandoned the *Advance*, and after a journey of eighty-four days in boats and sledges, after many narrow escapes and much privation they reached Upernavik on the 9th of August, where they were found by Captain Hartstene, commanding the *Release* and steamer *Arctic*, an expedition which had been fitted out by the United States to find and rescue them. Dr. Kane, in a scientific point of view, attained most important results, among some of them may be mentioned the following:

1. The discovery of a large channel to the northwest, free of ice, and leading into an open and expanding area, equally free.

2. The discovery and delineation of a large tract of land, forming the extension northward of the American continent.

3. The completion of the circuit of the straits and bay heretofore known at their southernmost opening of Smith's Sound.

The expedition finally reached New York, on its return, in October, 1855, having spent two winters in the Polar regions. A remarkable feature of this expedition was that the existence of the open Polar Sea which it discovered, had been already maintained by Dr. Kane, in a paper read before the American Geographical Society, October 14th, 1852. Well deserved honors were showered upon the lion hearted explorer. Gold medals were awarded to him by Congress, by the Legislature of New York, and by the Royal Geographical Society of London. He also received the Queen's medal given to Arctic explorers between the years 1818 and 1856, and a testimonial from the British residents of New York city.

HAYES' EXPEDITION.

Dr. Isaac I. Hayes, who accompanied the enterprise just referred to, and a firm believer in the theory of the open Polar Sea, succeeded with the aid of private subscriptions in organizing and fitting out another Arctic exploring expedition. With a company of only fourteen men he left Boston July 6, 1860, in the schooner *United States* for Proven and Upernavik, in Greenland, arriving at the latter place on the 12th of August, where he took on board three Danes, three Esquimaux and a number of dogs for sledge work. Hayes entered Baffin's Bay about the 20th of August, but was so delayed by ice that although he had designed reaching some point between latitude 79° and 80°, the schooner was frozen in at Port Foulke, a point about latitude 78°. Several sledge journeys were made during the winter months, but were somewhat barren of results until April 3, when with several sledges drawn by dogs, a lifeboat upon another sledge drawn by men, and twelve of his crew, he started across Smith's Sound to Grinnell Land to explore its coast line. After encountering great danger and difficulty, sending back nearly all the party, several sledges and the lifeboat, which could not be carried further, Hayes with three men reached Cape Hawks, Grinnell Land, on May the 11th. Turning northwards, they explored the coast for several days, but the men were exhausted, and Hayes was obliged to leave two of them on the way. With Knorr, his remaining companion, Dr. Hayes reached latitude 81° 35' on May 18, 1861, further advance being forbidden by the rotten ice and cracks. Having no boat the explorer retraced his steps, and taking up in detail the men he had dropped out *en route*, he reached the schooner in the beginning of June, after a toilsome journey, when, finding that she was so much damaged as to render further extended exploration impossible, he returned to Boston in October, 1861, fully determined to make another effort, which the civil war prevented him from undertaking.

CAPTAIN HALL.

This expedition, the last sent out from American shores, and the one, which in spite of its unfortunate conclusion, did more towards the solution of the points in question and the advancement of scientific knowledge than any of its predecessors, left Newfoundland, June 29th, 1871, sailed up Smith's Sound, and reached the 80th parallel about the end of August. Thence it proceeded up Kennedy Channel, and penetrated into Robeson Channel, its northern prolongation, and only thirteen miles wide. This passage was followed to 82° 16′ north latitude, being the highest point up to that time attained by any ship. Thence she returned to winter in Thank-God Harbor, a point on Robeson Channel latitude 81° 38. During the early autumn of the same year, Captain Hall made a sledge journey northwards, reaching latitude 82° 3′, and returning from this journey was taken ill and died November 8th, 1871, when Captain Buddington, the former sailing master, succeeded to the command. The *Polaris* left her winter quarters in August, 1872, and on October 15, 1872, being fast in the ice about latitude 78° 20′ and leaking badly, a part of the crew, while landing provisions, were separated from her by the breaking up of the ice floe, and drifted rapidly southward. On April 30, 1873, they were picked up by the ship *Tigress*—sent out by the United States to find and rescue them—in latitude 53° 35′ north The remainder of the crew who were left on the *Polaris* were rescued June 23d, 1873, by the Scotch steamer *Ravenscraig*, about latitude 75° 30′.

CAPTAIN NARES.

It may not be out of place here to give a brief outline of the last expedition which has returned from the Polar basin, and thus bring down to the present date the records of Arctic research, more especially as the route which it took was that followed by Kane, Hayes and Hall. The *Alert* and *Discovery*, under Captains Nares and Stephenson, sailed from England in May, 1875, and left Upernavik in Greenland July 22d of the same year. Passing through Smith's Sound and Kennedy Channel, the *Discovery* wintered in latitude 81° 44′, but the *Alert* struggled on through Robeson Channel, rounded the northeast point of Grantland, and found not, as was anticipated, a continuous coast line, but a vast ice bound sea. Finding no harbor, the ship was secured inside a barrier of ice in latitude 82° 31′, the most northerly wintering place ever yet occupied by man. The winter which followed was the severest on record. For 142 days the sun was never seen, and the mercury was frozen during a period of nearly nine weeks. Upon one occasion the thermometer showed 104° below the freezing point, and during two fearful weeks the mean temperature was 91° below the freezing point. As soon as the sun reappeared sledge exploration began. One party went east, exploring the northern shore of Greenland, and the other explored westward on the shores of Grantland. Captain Stephenson, of the *Discovery*, crossed Robeson Channel to Polaris Bay and erected over the grave of Captain Hall a tablet with a suitable inscription, which had been brought out from England for the purpose. The shores of Grantland were traced to longitude 85° 33', while those of Greenland were explored as far east as (west) longitude 50° 40'. Lastly, a party commanded by Commander Markham pushed northward, and after unheard of difficulties, on May 12, 1876, they planted the British flag in latitude 83° 20' 26", which is believed to be the most northern point ever reached by civilized man. After accomplishing these results the expedition returned to Great Britain, arriving at Valencia, Ireland, October 27th, 1876.

CAUSES OF FAILURE.

From this rapid survey of the more recent expeditions it will be seen that though Dr. Hayes, with only limited means at his command, and a small number of men made as high a latitude as 81° 35' in 1861: Captain Hall went only thirty-six nautical miles beyond him; while Captain Nares, with two vessels and over a hundred men, fitted out at a cost of a million of dollars, went only some seventy nautical miles beyond Captain Hall's furthest northern point. The records of Arctic exploration afford to the careful reader many details of great and exceeding interest, and none of these are more instructive than those which point the causes leading to the failure of so many expeditions planned with so much prudence and foresight, so thoroughly organized and so bravely led. Prominent amongst these causes may be named the following :

First. The expeditions were frequently sent out in the severest seasons, and at times when meteorological science, now so closely studied, was either in its infancy or entirely unknown, and could not be used to forecast the possibilities of closed or open seasons.

Second. Much valuable time—often the precious period during which alone the way was open and the temperature favorable—was lost by the explorers in making the voyage to the scene of their operations, which they reached, in many instances, only to find exploration impossible, and to be enclosed for whole seasons in the relentless ice, advance or retreat being alike impossible.

Third. The hardships of this voyage out, with its delays, too often so tried the men and sapped their strength that upon arriving in the Arctic basin they were unfitted for the work of exploration.

Fourth. The neglect or insufficient use of lime juice and other anti-scorbutics.

Fifth. The lack of proper discipline, which, in expeditions of this kind should be of the most thorough and perfect character.

Sixth. The failure to employ the Esquimaux as guides, hunters and assistants, and their invaluable dogs for draft purposes in the sledges.

Seventh. The imperfect means of communication—such, for instance, as signalling or telegraphing—between separated members or parties of the same expedition : and,

Eighth, and most important of all, a cause, fruitful of much disaster, which has sown in so many promising undertakings of the kind the seeds of dissension and of utter failure—dependence upon their vessels. Having their ships always near them, or within reach in case of need, as " cities of refuge"—having save them no fixed habitation, rendezvous or base of operations—with them they were timid, unadventurous and irresolute, while without them they were helpless and despairing.

And this brings us to the plan which is now proposed for adoption, a plan in which it is hoped to redeem the errors of the past by the knowledge of the present and the fair promise of the future. From the wrecks of former expeditions, with their tales of suffering and disaster, we should be able to pluck at last the weapon with which to conquer success. The days of spasmodic and unsupported expeditions have passed away, and a new era should open with the effort to commence the steady conquest, step by step—each step being used as the coign of vantage from which to plan and plant its successor—of the ice-bound cordon which environs the open sea, until the Columbus of Arctic discovery shall plow its virgin waters.

THE COLONIZATION PLAN.

The expedition of Captain Hall in the *Polaris*, in 1871, and of Captain Nares in the *Alert* and *Discovery*, in 1875, have shown that by the use of steam it is a comparatively easy matter to reach the entrance to Robeson's Channel in latitude 81° north, and that the serious difficulties to be overcome in reaching the Pole lie beyond that point. Parties from the two expeditions have made fair surveys 140 miles north of this, leaving only about 400 miles of unexplored regions between that and the goal of modern geographers—the Pole.

When Captain Hall reached the upper extremity of Robeson's Channel the lookout of the *Polaris* reported open water in sight and just beyond the pack which surrounded the vessel and prevented further progress. This open water was afterwards seen from the cape at the northern opening of Newman's Bay, and it was the opinion of the crew of that ill-fated vessel that if she had been but the fraction of an hour earlier in reaching the channel they could have steamed unobstructed over a veritable "open sea" to the Pole itself. We know that they did not succeed, but were forced to winter almost within sight of this sea, and subsequently, disheartened by the loss of their gallant commander, abandoned the enterprise.

Where this open water was found Captain Nares, in 1875 and 1876, found solid, impenetrable ice, through which no vessel could force its way, and over which it was equally impossible for sledge parties to work.

These facts appear to show that within the Arctic circle the seasons vary as markedly as in more temperate southern latitudes, and that the icy barriers to the Pole are sometimes broken up by favoring winds and temperature. To reach the Pole prompt advantage must be taken of such favoring circumstances, and to do this with the greatest certainty and with the least expenditure of time, money, and human life, it is essential that the exploring party be on the ground at the very time the ice gives way and opens the gateway to the long sought prize. This can only be done by colonizing a few hardy, resolute, and experienced men at some point near the borders of the Polar Sea, and the most favorable one for the purpose appears to be that where the Discovery wintered last year.

Such a party should consist of at least fifty men, and should be provided with provisions and other necessary supplies for three years, at the end of which period they should be visited, and if still unsuccessful in accomplishing the object, revictualled and again left to their work. Captain Hall spent eight years among the Esquimaux, and each year found himself better fitted to withstand the severity of the Arctic circle, and the party of which I speak would in like manner become acclimated, and eventually succeed in accomplishing the long-sought end. With a strong, substantial building, such as could easily be carried on shipboard, the party could be made as comfortable and as safe from atmospheric dangers as are the men of the signal service stationed on the summits of Pike's Peak and Mount Washington, or the employés of the Hudson's Bay Company stationed at Fort York, where a temperature of minus 60 degrees is not uncommon. A good supply of medicine, a skillful surgeon, and such fresh provision as could be found by hunting parties would enable them to keep off scurvy, and to maintain as good a sanitary condition as the inhabitants of Godhaven, in Greenland. Game was found in fair quantities by the *Polaris* party on the Greenland coast, and by those from the *Alert* and *Discovery* on the mainland to the west, especially in the vicinity of the last-named vessel, where fifty-four musk oxen were killed during the season, with quantities of other and smaller game. A seam of good coal was also found by the *Discovery's* party, which would render the question of fuel a light one, and thus remove one of the greatest difficulties hitherto found by Arctic voyagers.

The principal depot or post is to be located upon Lady Frankin Bay between latitude 81° and 82°, and there is no question that this can be reached with a steam vessel, as Captain Hall went as high as Cape Union, between latitude 82° and 83° with the *Polaris*, and Captain Nares still higher with the *Alert*. It is probable that the last named point may be reached with the vessel, in which case coal and provisions could be deposited there to form a secondary base of operations for the exploring party. If this latter can be done the road to the Pole will be shortened by about ninety miles in distance and three weeks or more in time, two very important items. It should be clearly understood, that the only use to be made of the vessel, which it is hoped to obtain from the Navy Department, is in the transportation of the men and supplies to the location of the colony. When this is done the vessel will return to the United States and await further instructions. An annual visit might be made to the colony, to carry fresh food and supplies, to keep its members informed of events occurring in the outside world, and bear them news and letters from anxious relatives, to bring back news of progress made and of a private character to friends; also, if necessary, to bring back invalided members of the expedition, and carry out fresh colonists to take their places. This annual visit, however, is not absolutely necessary, for if the return trip is deferred until the third year, it is probable that the work of the colony will be found completed, and it can be permanently abandoned. The vessel should, of course, take out a sufficient quantity of supplies to enable the colony to remain longer than three years if necessary. It is hoped that Congress will authorize the employment of detailed officers and men to form the majority of the colony, as this plan will best secure that military discipline, without which the failure of former expeditions will undoubtedly find a new parallel in this last one. The permanent colony shall consist of fifty selected men, mustered into the service of the United States, three commisisoned officers, and two surgeons; all to be selected with a view to their especial fitness for the work, young, able bodied, resolute men, who can be depended upon to carry out instructions to the extreme limit of human endurance. An astronomer and two or more naturalists, to be selected by the National Academy of Sciences, and to work under instructions from that body, but subject to such general supervision and direction from the head of the expedition, as is customary at all posts in charge of an officer of the United States, should accompany the expedition. One or more members of the regular force should be competent to make meteorological observations, and to communicate by telegraph and signals whenever such communication becomes necessary.

ESQUIMAUX AND DOGS.

To the expeditionary corps brought from the United States should be added a number of Esquimaux to serve as hunters, guides, &c., and who can be taken over with their families from Disco or Upernavik, in Greenland, and also an ample number of the Esquimaux dogs, so indispensable for sledging and so useful as food when their capacity for work is gone.

The outfit of the *Polaris* expedition offers a safe guide in this respect, and one which, if followed, will afford proper safeguards against scurvy. Lime juice has been used too often and has proved too absolute an antidote for its virtues to be called in question now.

THE COLONY

should be kept under the strictest discipline, and to this end should be formally enrolled in the military service, save perhaps the strictly scientific members. By discipline only can such control be exercised as will be indispensable to the successful ending of the search.

One cannot read without pain the account of the *Polaris'* expedition, where the bonds of discipline, only too loose before Hall's untimely death, were entirely relaxed after it. The first in command of the new expedition should be a man able not only to gauge men but to control them, and his second should be like unto him. Enthusiasm and energy are especially desirable, but coolness of temper, firmness of rule, persistency of purpose, and a well balanced mind, fertile in resources and expedients, are indispensable to success.

The outfit of the expedition should include some two hundred miles or more of copper wire, to connect the colony at Lady Franklin Bay with the subsidiary depot at Cape Union, and thence northward as far as practicable. Copper wire is strong, light, flexible and a good conductor, and can be worked while lying upon the dry snow or ice without support. The necessary battery, material and instruments should be taken to equip the amount of line, and the battery could be kept permanently at the Bay station, where, fuel being abundant, it could be kept from freezing. A few sets of signal equipments, such as are used in the army signal service, would also form an indispensable part of the outfit, and all of the men should be instructed in their use and in the signal code. Thus provided with means of communication the sledging parties could move forward with confidence, as they would be able, when necessary, to call upon their comrades who remained behind for advice or assistance. Open water will, it is believed, be found in any ordinary season before the party gets as far north as 83° 20′

26″, the turning point of Lieutenant Markham's sledge party, and that boats can thence be used to the land which it is still believed will be found about latitude 85°, in accordance with Captain Hall's theory based upon the native traditions. The existence of coal at the *Discovery's* winter quarters settles the question of colonization and the location of the colony as a means of Polar exploration; and the Nares expedition would have been a success if it had done nothing more than this. The failure of his admirably equipped expedition is in a great measure attributable to the abnormally cold season and the exceptionable character of the winds, which had resulted in the formation of ice ridges running across the line of march, thus making progress difficult, slow and dangerous. It is reasonable to suppose from past meteorological records that these unusual conditions will not exist during the present season, and, indeed, may not occur again for several years. Instead of discouraging further effort, the failure of Nares' expedition from the causes named should stimulate fresh endeavors, and hold out a fair prospect of success. At any rate, the little colony on Lady Franklin Bay during their three years' residence, besides having the opportunity of *selecting* an open season, and becoming thoroughly hardened and acclimated, would have their work narrowed down to a common focus—the pathway due north. The work of the Nares expedition clears the way for a direct movement upon the Pole. The explorations westward along the coast by Lieutenant Aldrich, and eastward by Lieutenant Beaumont, obviate the necessity for similar work now. Upon landing and unloading the stores and provisions quarters should be erected, and the vessel, returning to the United States, would leave behind her a thoroughly equipped, self supporting and self reliant colony which would push, ever northward, the limits of discovery.

SLEDGE JOURNEYS.

The attempt to draw the loaded sledges by means of mere manual labor should not be made unless it should become in any particular instance a matter of absolute necessity, as it is sure to result disastrously, and seems to have been one of the causes of failure of the Nares expedition. The expedition from the colony to the Pole may consist of eight sledges, with six men to each sledge, the distance to be traveled being some 400 miles, divided into eight stages of fifty miles each. At the end of the first stage one sledge could be sent back. A portion of the provisions which it originally carried would have been consumed, and the rest would have been deposited in a *cache* in the ice secure from Arctic animals. At the end of the second stage the second sledge would be sent back; at the close of the third stage the third sledge would take up its homeward journey, and, following out this plan, only a single sledge would remain. The returning sledges being but lightly freighted, and traveling, moreover, a route already pioneered, several of their hands could be retained so as to man the eighth sledge with ten or more explorers. This last sledge with its full complement would perform the most important work of all. It would press forward, reach the Pole, make the necessary observations and then return. Upon its homeward journey it would follow the route already made in the forward journey, and would find provisions at each successive *cache*. This portion of the plan would be useful in a closed season, but in an open one the journey would have to be made either wholly in boats or partly in these and partly by sledges.

ADVANTAGES OF THE SMITH'S SOUND ROUTE.

This route is preferable to that by Spitzbergen, where the ice drift is much greater and where the all important vein of coal does not exist. Moreover, two recent expeditions, those of Hall and Nares, have shown that the whole length of the Sound is practicable for steaming up as far as Discovery Harbor, on Lady Franklin Bay, if not beyond, in any ordinarily open season. But it is not doubted that during its three years' sojourn the colony may experience and take advantage of such a season as will carry an expedition much farther, and perhaps even the whole distance to the Pole. There is a *warm* current setting steadily northward from the Pacific Ocean through Behring's Straits, which constitutes the mighty ocean river of the Kuro Siwo. This current must have an outlet, which is possibly found in the southerly drift of the Atlantic side.

During the summer there are probably long lanes of water free of ice, from the upper end of Smith's Sound, and following these, against the downward flowing current, a pathway will surely be found, practicable for boats, during some favoring season. Such favoring season and such a practicable pathway can only be found by men colonized as proposed at a point where—half the journey already safely completed—they will be ready, healthy, vigorous, acclimated and unwearied by a long and perilous voyage—they will be ready and eager to seize the proffered opportunity. Failing such an opportunity, a chance barely possible, the alternative of sledge journeys stills remains, and sledge journeys undertaken under better and more favorable auspices than any which have been as yet attempted.

THE HEALTH AND PROSPECTS OF A COLONY.

The severity of the climate on Lady Franklin Bay and in the neighboring regions has been much exaggerated. To parties under cover it is not more trying than that at the summits of Mount Washington, in New Hampshire, or of Pike's Peak, in Colorado, as stated by a former member of one of Dr. Hayes' expeditions, who has since served a year upon the summit of the last named mountain. The report on the *Polaris* expedition shows that during the summer all the low lands and elevations at Thank God Harbor (opposite Discovery Harbor on Lady Franklin Bay) were bare of snow and ice, excepting patches here and there in the shade of the rocks. The soil at that period was covered with a vegetation of moss interspersed with small plants and willows. Seals were abundant in the water, as were also jelly-fish and shrimps. Captain Hall's last despatch, dated from his encampment on the north side of Newman's Bay, nearly a whole degree further north than the site of the proposed colony, says: "We find this a much warmer country than we expected. We found the mountains on either side of Kennedy Channel and Robeson Strait entirely bare of snow and ice with the exception of one glacier that we saw. The country abounds with life, and seals, game, ducks, musk cattle, rabbits, wolves, foxes, bears, partridges, &c. Our sealers have shot two seals in the open water while at this encampment."

Again, there are several towns in Northern Asia inside the Arctic circle, and a flourishing city of Russia (Archangel) is not far from it. At Yakutsk, on the river Lena, the ground is frozen solid all the year round, and only thaws a few inches in depth during the hottest summer. The thermometer often falls to 65° or 70° *minus*, and every winter there are periods of two or three weeks during which it does not rise above 60° *minus* upon Farenheit's scale. Yet this is a town possessing a population of 4,000 hardy, prosperous and contented human beings.

HOME SICKNESS.

The members of former exploring parties sailed away from the hospitable shores of Christendom, leaving behind them no connecting link of succor or of aid. With proud yet foreboding hearts, wafted by favoring gales, they passed into the very shadows of death.

Nostalgia, that dreaded foe of isolated men, found in them an easy prey through the long, sunless, Arctic night, and drove some to mutiny and others to suicide, while, when the hour of deadly peril came—the supreme moment of despair —the stoutest heart was appalled by the knowledge that succor, if sent at all, must be guided by the merest chance, and that the rude cairn which covered his last resting place or his frozen effigy upon some drifting ice-floe might never meet the gaze of human eye. The new enterprise will go forth under far different auspices to seek a definite rendez-vouz from which every forward step will be duly chronicled, and the members of the expedition, well knowing that communication will be kept up for their aid, comfort and supply, will strive with a keener endeavor for the long coveted prize.

But changing seasons with their varying temperatures bring with them varying conditions of existence. There is a brighter side to the picture, and Dr. Hayes gives encouraging views upon this point, urging the general cheerfulness of Arctic crews, which is such a great stimulant to health and to success. Speaking of his expedition in 1861, he says that the crew were always, and had been, in perfect health ; that he was his own ship's doctor, and a doctor without a patient, and that, "believing in Democritus rather than Heraclitus, they had laughed the scurvy and all other sources of ill-health to shame." Nor is the danger of Arctic exploration so great as it, at first thought, appears to be. A distinguished naval officer who has served in those regions states that, "of all the seas visited by men-of-war the Arctic have proved the most healthy ;" and Mr. Posthumus states, further, that, since 1841, England and America have sent out thirty-two expeditions, the total number of deaths from which has been only 38 men, or 1.7 per cent., a percentage which would appear much more favorable if the expeditions of the Germans, Swedes and Norwegians were included.

FACTS FROM FORMER EXPEDITIONS, AND VIEWS OF SCIENTISTS AND EXPLORERS, WHICH SHOW THE PLAN TO BE A FEASIBLE ONE.

The expedition of Captain Nares, while a failure in certain respects, has done a vast service for future explorers in clearly defining the difficulties to be met and overcome. The coast on either side of Robeson's Channel has been so well laid down as to render any further attempts in this direction futile on the part of an expedition *via* Smith's Sound. In that direction the Pole must be reached by sledge and boat from Cape Joseph Henry, which is but 7° from the Pole.

Captain Nares, who certainly does not underrate the difficulties, states that Lady Franklin Bay, latitude 81° 45', can be reached every year if the attempt is made in the right season.

There it is proposed that the colony shall be established and left for three years. Its high latitude, the facility for reaching it and the seam of coal found by the *Discovery*, render it undoubtedly the best wintering place in Robeson's Channel. The party having three years to remain and no means of retreat open, has every inducement to devote its time and energy to the accomplishment of its purpose. From Cape Joseph Henry to the Pole is about 430 miles, which in a favorable season could be passed over in ninety days, going and returning.

In 1853 Captain McClintock made a sledge trip of 1,200 miles in 106 days, and Lieutenant Mecham one of over 1,000 in ninety-three days. In 1821 a trip of 800 miles was made by Wrangell in thirty-six days. The character of the ice passed over by him accords, in his description, with that found by Commander Markham. It is true that Commander Markham's party only averaged one and a fourth miles daily, but several causes operated against more rapid progress.

First. The want of dogs. The failure to take them seems a great error, for when their capacity for work is gone they can be used for food.

Second. The pack ice was exceedingly rough, and the drifted snow lay in such directions as to seriously impede their progress. The snow lay in its particular direction from a continued west wind, which does not prevail every year.

The evidence of Arctic travelers all shows that the surface of the ice materially changes from year to year, being some years quite smooth. The statements of Lieutenant Payer, the commander of the Austro-Hungarian expedition, 1872–74, are especially important in this respect, he giving an account of the change from smooth, regular fields of ice to rough, huge, disjointed packs.

Third. The party leaving land in Robeson's Channel presumably experienced some drift south until they had cleared the 83d ,parallel, when the tendency is divided between drifting east or south. The tide and current observations in Robeson's Channel showed continued strong southerly currents. The experience of Parry, who traveled weeks on pack ice before he discovered the general movement, shows how imperceptible the drift is. The statement that Commander Markham's party traveled 276 miles to go seventy-three miles from the ship and but 245 to return corroborates this opinion. The party was thirty-nine days going and, although sick, but thirty-three days returning. Directly north of Cape Joseph Henry the drift must become feebler as a party goes north, as Robeson's Channel being too small to relieve the Polar basin of all its ice, the general drift is east, so as to escape by the east coast of Greenland. Any drift apart from the locality near the mouth of Robeson's Channel would hardly increase one's distance from the Pole.

Fourth. The party was unprovided with lime juice or other anti-scorbutics, and incipient scurvey impaired the strength of the party shortly after starting.

It is exceedingly probable that Commander Markham's party, when compelled by scurvy to turn back, was very near to land. The water had, we are told, shallowed to seventy fathoms.

Dr. Peterman, who probably has examined with the closest attention the records of all Polar expeditions, is firmly of the opinion that land will be found directly north of Cape Joseph Henry, in about latitude 87°. That land was not seen by Markham's. party in no wise militates against this theory, as the nature of the ice was such as to preclude a view of even eight or ten miles, and low land, such as usually prevails in the Arctic regions, can for the greater part of the year only be distinguished from pack ice by being traveled over. Should land be found within one hundred and fifty miles of Cape Joseph Henry a sub-station could be stocked with provisions, and success thus rendered a certainty. Should the sea open, the crossing of it would be a matter of only a few days. That it does open for a considerable distance Captain Nares admits in his report as definitely settled. The undoubted evidence of Kane, Hayes, Meyer, and Payer, is conclusive on this point. The latter, at Cape Fligely, latitude 82° 5', in 1874, found a sea open as far as eye could reach. An English writer commenting on this account ingenuously remarks that Payer was too scientific, too cool, and possessed of too good judgment to term it an open sea, but called it a "polymia," or water hole. It matters naught what it is named so long as it affords a safe, open road for a considerable distance toward the Pole. Dr. Petermann, the great geographer, believes such to be the case, and doubts not but had Captain Nares remained another year he would have reached the Pole.

Ferrell, the great mathematical physicist, states that the physical condition of the globe forbids our believing in a solid frozen sea, but that the ocean currents maintain an open sea of greater or less extent. This opinion is borne out by the tidal and current observation made in Smith's Sound and Robeson's Channel and by the authorities quoted above, and also by the fact that, in June, 1872, the *Polaris* found open water to nearly 83°, while Payer, in the *Tegetthoff*, was fast in the ice at 76°, near Nova Zembla; and, lastly, in 1837 the *True Love*, of Hull, England, sailed north of Nova Zembla to latitude 82° 30', and saw an open sea as far as eye could reach.

A SUMMARY.

To sum up, then, in brief: It is proposed to ascend a well known and practicable channel to an equally well known point where exploring parties have previously wintered, and there form a colony. From the post so formed no time will be spent in needless quests along the shore either east or west, as surveys there have already been completed; but starting afresh, the point of *their beginning* having the closing point of former expeditions, with all the information of their forerunners to commence with; better provisioned, equipped and disciplined; with better means of inter-communication; thoroughly acclimated, and without the refuge of the ship to paralyze energy and sow the seeds of discontent and slothfulness; with all these advantages of greater nearness to the coveted goal, and more favorable conditions for its attainment, it is proposed to await the favorable opportunity, born of the varying seasons, and follow it up to an assured success. In other words, to use alike the partial successes and the partial failures of others, added to the utmost foresight, experience and scientific aids to form the fulcrum of the archimedian lever which shall move the Arctic world.

PUBLIC OPINION.

Already applications to serve have been received from many, most of them men who are in every way qualified for the work, and the press throughout the country are almost unanimous in urging the adoption of the plan. The American Geographical Society, the Smithsonian Institution, the National Academy of Science, the members of former Arctic expeditions and many gentlemen of high distinction in the walks of science have given it their cordial support, while several of the most important cities throughout the country have directed their Representatives in Congress to advocate the passage of the bill.

INTERNATIONAL CO-OPERATION.

If America would not be outdone by other nations it behooves her to move at once The English press report Sweedish and Dutch expeditions as already organizing. The English themselves, although they have knighted Captain Nares and promoted every commanding officer of that expedition, are by no means satisfied with their failure or partial success, and the government is being urged to send out again the vessels just returned. France is about to organize a new Arctic expedition, and already there comes across the ocean a suggestion from both France and Holland that by mutual agreement a series of synchronous observations should be taken by each expedition at all points of their courses for future comparison and for the advancement of science throughout the world. The colony on Lady Franklin Bay would form a rallying point and center for the different expeditions of various nations, and it would be the natural objective point of those trying to reach the Pole by way of Behring's Straits and Nova Zembla, of which there are several, while for those going by way of Smith's Sound it would form the natural base of operations. By the adoption of this plain, therefore, the United States would hold the key to the position and the Pole, a position as glorious as it would be difficult, and one equally worthy of our national greatness and enterprise. Certainly, having once put our hands to the plow, we should not turn back. Having done so nobly in the past we can not afford to idly relinquish all part in the future. Such a course would neither be consistent with our reputation for energy nor creditable to our Government.

CONGRESSIONAL AID.

The sum ($50,000) asked from Congress is small, and we have enough of surplus energy in either the army or navy to furnish a force in every way fitted for the work. The present Secretary of the Navy has always taken the most hearty interest in Arctic explorations, and would probably find a vessel fitted to do its specified work, and from army and navy could come qualified volunteers.

In reading over the following bill which has been introduced in the present Congress and referred to the Committee on Naval Affairs, several points will immediately present themselves : the sum asked for is small, almost to pettiness; the plan of detailing officers and others already in the Government service ; the use of a vessel which would otherwise perhaps be idle or out of commission ; and the fact that the money is not to be used in fitting out a mere Arctic expedition, but to *establish a colony.* It must be borne in mind that out of four purely American expeditions, three were mainly equipped by private enterprise, while the fourth, that of Captain Hall, which the United States equipped at the paltry cost of some $50,000, achieved, in fact, more than had hitherto been done by the same or any other route, and little less than England accomplished later at a cost of $1,000,000. The present plan is designed to hold the point *which Hall attained* as a *permanent post* for a series of years, from whence to make further advances.

In the House of Representatives, January 8, 1877. Read twice, referred to the Committee on Naval Affairs, and ordered to be printed.

Mr. Hunter, on leave, introduced the following bill : A bill to authorize and equip an expedition to the Arctic Seas.

Be it enacted by the Senate and House of Representatives of the United States of America in Congress assembled, That the President of the United States be authorized to organize and send out one or more expeditions toward the North Pole, and to establish a temporary colony, for the purposes of exploration, at some point north of the eighty-first degree of north latitude, on or near the shore of Lady Franklin Bay: to detail such officers or other persons of the public service to take part in the same as may be necessary, and to use any public vessel that may be suitable for the purpose; the scientific operations of the expedition to be prosecuted in accordance with the advice of the National Academy of Science; and that the sum of fifty thousand dollars, or such part thereof as may be necessary, be hereby appropriated out of any moneys in the Treasury not otherwise appropriated, to be expended under the direction of the President: *Provided*, that no part of the sum so appropriated shall be carried to the surplus fund or covered into the Treasury until the purpose of the appropriation shall have been completed, but may be applied to expenses of said expedition incurred during any subsequent year that said expedition may be engaged in its duties.

CONCLUSION.

An attempt has been made in the foregoing pages to give a bare outline of the chart which points the way to Arctic conquests; but who shall preach the crusade? Surely some chivalrous spirit in the halls of Congress will raise the glove which the English have so recently flung down, and accept the friendly challenge to a noble contest! During the late bitter civil war, which arrested the footsteps of the gallant Hayes upon the threshold of further discovery, and through which our ship of state rode so triumphantly to port, the hand of the Architect was not stayed or the mason's chisel raised from the marble pile where, from her snowy dome, the Goddess of Liberty looks forth with earnest eyes for newer realms of conquest, and there can be no time more fitting than the present—a time of more peaceful contest—for the prayer of science to find a hearing and an answer. It is to be hoped that some such champion will be found, brave and patriotic enough to forget the acrimonies of the present in the glories of the past, and, rising above the political discussions of the hour, to identify himself with an international undertaking which shall reflect glory upon himself and clothe the country of our pride with added honor!

The United States has entered the lists in this matter upon too many occasions, it has spent too much treasure, it has sacrificed too many valuable lives to draw back now.

And yet we have fairly shared the honors of Arctic explorations with our English cousins; and their last effort was, in fact, more discouraging than our own. We have spent but a fraction of the treasure and sacrificed the merest tithe of the lives which have been given by England to this great and noble quest, and yet the results which we have achieved will not yield to those attained by any other nation in point of importance or of permanence. We need entertain no doubts of the result. Through the dim vista of vanished centuries the oar of colonizing Greek, the sword of conquering Roman have descended to the Anglo-Saxon as his peculiar appanage and possession, while the heart of Asia, the deserts of Africa and the mighty cañons of the West bear ample testimony with the ice-bound seas that neither peaceful implement nor warlike weapon have been found too heavy for the brawny hand of the youngest scion of the English speaking race.

But the rock-bound coast, the lonely glacier, teach their lesson of Christian fortitude and of dauntless courage to no unwilling ears. The English ensign still floats in those vast solitudes, planted in advance of ours, and the tablet placed over the grave of Hall by English hands is not only a graceful courtesy, but a friendly challenge to sojourn once more in those waste and desert places whence the noble Hall, like the Jewish seer of old, looked forth upon the land of promise which his feet might never tread—a land not flowing, indeed, with milk and honey, but rich in the aurora-tinted gifts of science. The memorial tablet, the lonely grave, still keep watch and ward above the conquests we have won, while from beneath, the Arctic martyr beckons with a ghostly hand to future glory, and taking up again our keen unrusted weapons, we should never pause until one more star is added to the galaxy which adorns our flag—the mighty planet that in silent majesty guards, in those dim and distant regions, the solemn mysteries of the Pole.

APPENDIX.

The following selections are made from the numerous communications received favoring the "Colonization" plan in its most essential features, and show the general feeling of interest in the subject among explorers and men of science.

In one feature several of the gentlemen whose views are given differ with me—that of the permanent retention of a vessel at the proposed colony. This, in my opinion, would be unwise and fatal to the success of the expedition, as I have explained elsewhere.

(From the President of the American Geographical Society.)

AMERICAN GEOGRAPHICAL SOCIETY,
No. 11 W. 29TH ST., NEW YORK CITY,
January 18th, 1877.

Captain H. W. Howgate:

MY DEAR SIR: Before your letter was received I inserted in my annual address a notice of your plan and of the bill before Congress.

As you will find by my address, your mode of exploration is the one that I have uniformly approved and recommended for many years. I expressed this opinion in my address of 1869, and in the first of my addresses, which have been printed, (1870,) I declared my conviction that a passage to the Pole by water would, in all probability, not be found, and that the true method of exploration was by sledge operations upon land from the furthest point that could be safely reached by a vessel.

*   *   *   *   *   *   *   *

You will see from this that I have long been impressed with your general plan, and the only criticism I have to offer is that I think the station should not be limited to some point north of 81°; for though a vessel may winter securely in Discovery Bay, and although there is a fine seam of bituminous coal three miles from where the *Discovery* wintered, yet the region, as shown by the experience of the English expedition and by the abandonment of the Esquimaux settlements just below it, is very barren of animal

28

life either upon the land or upon the water, whilst at Fort Foulke it is otherwise, and a temporary colony could be maintained there without any difficulty. For this reason I think it would have been better to have said north of 78°.

It will afford me great pleasure to do all that I can to forward your views, and anything that the Society can do I am sure will be done.

The suggestion I have made as to the limitation in the bill as to location of colony is entirely for your consideration, and will in no way affect our hearty support of the measure.
* * * * * * * *

Very truly yours,

CHAS. P. DALY.

(From Prof. Elias Loomis, of Yale College.)

YALE COLLEGE, *January* 14, 1877.

Capt. H. W. Howgate:

DEAR SIR: I have received your letter of January 7th, together with a copy of a bill to be presented to Congress, asking for an appropriation to defray the expense of another expedition towards the North Pole. I have for many years taken a deep interest in Polar expeditions, and see no reason for abandoning further effort because former expeditions have not accomplished all that was expected. If we review the entire history of Polar expeditions since Captain Parry's first voyage, more than half a century ago, we find that every expedition has proved in some sense a failure; that is, has accomplished less than was anticipated; and some may therefore conclude that all the labor which has been expended on this Polar problem has been wasted. I take a very different view of the subject, and consider that the results of the many Polar expeditions, from the first voyage of Capt. Parry to the present time, are worth far more than all the money and labor which have been expended on them.

In order to estimate the value of the results of these expeditions we should consider what would have been the state of our knowledge of the physics of the globe if no such expeditions had been undertaken. There is scarcely a problem relating to the physics of the globe which can be fully understood without a knowledge of the phenomena within the Polar regions. Whatever phenomena we may wish to investigate, it is of special importance to determine its maximum and minimum values, and in nearly all questions of terrestrial physics one or other of these values is found in the neighborhood of the Pole. If, for example, we wish to determine the distribution of temperature upon the surface of the globe, it is specially important to determine the extremes of temperature, one of which is to be found near the equator and the other near the Poles. If we wish to investigate the system of circulation of the winds, our investigation would be sadly defficient without a knowledge of the phenomena in the Polar regions.

If we wish to study the fluctuations in the pressure of the atmosphere, whether periodical or accidental, we cannot be sure that we understand the phenomena in the middle latitudes unless we know what takes place in the Polar regions. If we wish to investigate the currents of the ocean, we find indications of currents coming from the Polar regions, and it is important to be able to trace these currents to their source. If we wish to investigate the laws of the tides, we need observations from every ocean ; and observations in the Arctic regions have a special value on account of their distance from the place where the daily tidal wave takes its origin. If we wish to study the phenomena of atmospheric electricity and of auroral exhibitions, no part of the world is more important than the Polar regions. If we wish to study the phenomena of terrestrial magnetism, observations in the Polar regions have a special value, since it is here the dipping needle assumes a vertical position and the intensity of the earth's magnetism is the greatest. If we wish to determine the dimensions and figures of the earth, we require to know the length of a degree of latitude where it is greatest and also where it is least. If we wish to determine how the force of gravity varies in different parts of the world, we require observations of the second's pendulum both where it is greatest and where it is least. In short, there is no problem connected with the physics of the globe which does not demand observations from the Polar regions, and generally the Poles and the Equator are more important as stations of observation than any other portions of the earth's surface. If the information which has been acquired upon the various subjects in the numerous Polar expeditions of the last half century were annihilated, it would leave an immense chasm which would greatly impair the value of the researches which have been made in other parts of the world.

The subjects to which I have here referred are scientific

rather than commercial; but many of them have an important bearing upon questions which affect the commerce of the globe. In the attempts which are now being made by the joint efforts of the principal nations of the globe to determine the laws of storms, if we could have daily observations from a group of stations within the Arctic circle, it is believed that they would prove of the highest value in enabling us to explain the phenomena of the middle latitudes. Every winter upon the eastern side of the Rocky Mountains we find an intensely cold wave moving down from the northward and spreading over a large portion of the United States. How can we fully understand the cause of the great changes of temperature which so frequently occur during the winter months unless we know where this cold air comes from? And how can this be determined without fixed stations of observation extending northward over the Polar regions?

The vast extension of the commerce of the world in recent times and its increased security are due in no small degree to more accurate information respecting the physics of the globe, including such subjects as the mean direction and force of the prevalent winds; the laws of storms; the use of the barometer in giving warning of approaching violent winds; the surest mode of escaping the violence of a storm when overtaken by a gale; the most advatnageous route from one part to another; the direction and velocity of the current in every ocean; the variation of the magnetic needle in all latitudes, and its changes from year to year; together with many other problems; and most of these investigations have been greatly facilitated by observations which have been made within the Arctic regions. I do not regard it as any exaggeration to claim that the benefits which have resulted both directly and indirectly to the commerce of the world in consequence of Polar expeditions, are more than equal to all the money which has been expended on these enterprises.

Is any additional advantage to the commerce of the world to be anticipated from further explorations in the Polar regions? Undoubtedly. Precisely what these advantages may prove to be we cannot certainly pronounce beforehand; but upon most of the questions to which I have already alluded more minute information is needed. The demands of science are by no means satisfied, and we may confidently anticipate that any advance in our scientific knowledge respecting questions connected with the physics of the globe will impart increased security to commerce. If a steamer starting from New York and traveling northward could pass directly over the North Pole, through Behring Straits into the Pacific Ocean it would be a triumph of geographical science equal to the first discovery of America. Whether such a result will ever be witnessed we cannot safely predict; but past explorations have not shown that such an achievement is impossible. I hope we shall not rest contented while so much that is clearly feasible remains to be done and until the northern boundary of Greenland has been traced.

Hoping that your efforts to secure assistance in the further prosecution of this Polar problem may prove successful,

I am, with much respect, yours truly,

ELIAS LOOMIS.

U. S. NAVAL OBSERVATORY,
WASHINGTON, D. C., *January* 25, 1877.

MY DEAR CAPTAIN: You have asked me for my views in regard to the vast methods of conducting Arctic exploration. I take great pleasure in complying with your request.

＊　　＊　　＊　　＊　　＊　　＊　　＊

I am opposed to all spasmodic efforts to reach the Pole, because the chances of success are not commensurate with the necessary outlay. There have been comparatively few well organized Polar expeditions, and all these have endeavored to effect their object in a single season by a spurt, as it were. They have gone at erratic intervals, knowing comparatively nothing of the laws that govern the Arctic seasons; so that, so far as their knowledge of the meteorological and hydrographical conditions of the Polar regions was concerned, each of them stood an equal chance of success. Under these circumstances each expedition was justly regarded as an experiment. The failures that attended them were, in a great measure, due to a blind haste to gain their objects. That eminent scientists should have considered the quite meagre results as an ample reward for the expenditure of life and money, proves only the magnitude and extent of the scientific secrets which are locked up in the frozen North awaiting the intelligent and persistent explorer. The only legacies that can be considered of absolute value which these expeditions have left to the world are the feats of heroism and endurance that send the enthusiastic glow of admiration through the heart of humanity, the bloodless deeds of renown, and the immortal glory won, not by triumphs over fellow men, but by victories over nature in its most forbidden guise.

*　　*　　*　　*　　*　　*　　*　　*

A ship bearing reinforcements and supplies should, if possible, visit the colony each year. No one should be compelled to remain longer than one winter either on the ship or at the station; and the commander should each year order home those whom experience has proved to be unserviceable or uncompanionable.

The band of explorers should spend each spring and autumn in making excursions in various directions and in paying minute attention to the accurate survey and delineation of the country traversed. Dogs should be used for draught. They are the natural teams of the country; they require little food and no clothing; they need no shelter; they are fleet and strong; they will serve as food to a famishing party, and, moreover, they multiply so amazingly that, with proper precautions, the kennel need never be empty. The sleds should approximate in shape, size and material to those used by the Esquimaux. At least they should be fastened together by thongs of raw hide and should be shod with ivory. Esquimaux should be employed as dog drivers to accompany all sledge expeditions, both because they understand how to take care of dogs, how to build, quickly and well, snowgloos (which are best suited for temporary shelter) and also because they know how to hunt, which is a very important consideration. Now, white men, with all their genius and skill, while able to do these things tolerably after considerable practice, are totally unable while on a sledge journey to make themselves as comfortable as the Esquimaux, who, at the same time, need less food and clothing. Hence, the knowledge and aid of these hardy sons of the North should be invoked. A man with ordinary tact and judgment can secure a willing service from these innocent and docile people.

*　　*　　*　　*　　*　　*　　*　　*

A continuous effort would also afford an opportunity to test men, and, in time, those qualified physically and mentally for the peculiar service would be secured. A long residence at the station or on the ship—whether continuous or broken by returns home for recuperation—would give an experience in the modes of Arctic travel that would be valuable indeed, and that would insure final success. The service would be eminently desirable, and each year hosts of volunteers would present themselves, from whom good men could be chosen. Under proper management scurvy would not appear, and if the quarters were comfortable and the food plentiful and of the right kind, the men could live as well and happily as in more southern latitudes.

In order to preserve the health of the crew, special attention should be paid to discipline. The men should not be required to expose themselves so as to become very cold or wet except under the most imperative necessity; neither should any unnecessary service, nor service of questionable expediency, be forced from them. The great solicitude of a commander of an Arctic expedition should be to keep up the spirits of his men, to banish all repinings and disquietude, and to promote their happiness and thorough content. Scurvy has no power over a man with a cheerful frame of mind if only he has the opportunity to provide suitably for the wants of his body. Exercise must be performed cheerfully and with the mind interested, to be of any service; enforced exercise rarely accomplishes the intended results.

*   *   *   *   *   *   *   *

Land as a base of operations is essential for the b of Polar effort, not only because thereby whatever advance may be made can be held, but because the value of the observations will be increased if made at a permanent station. Many routes present this advantage, and I would not presume to say, absolutely, which would offer the fewest obstacles to an advance to the Pole. I trust that in a few years every possible route will be faithfully tried.

But as an American and for an American expedition, I would unhesitatingly recommend the Smith's Sound route— the field in which Kane, Hayes and Hall won such renown— a field that still affords an opportunity to show the world what American pluck and enterprise can accomplish. It will be unnecessary to mention additional reasons for this preference. They will naturally present themselves to the Arctic student.

*   *   *   *   *   *   *   *

The United States has the right to consider the Smith's

Sound route as peculiarly its own, and no effort should be spared to carry on in that direction the work of her illustrious heroes, living and dead. Her history contains no brighter pages than those that record their courage and endurance.

* * * * * * * *

Your plan, so far as you have announced it, is so like mine that it seems almost unnecessary to say how heartily in sympathy I am with you in your efforts to organize a Polar expedition upon a sound basis. I trust that you will be very successful; that Congress will determine to carry on the good work, and that you will be spared to share its triumphs. Polar research offers more rewards in the way of national glory and renown than any other similar enterprise.

I am fully convinced that the flag of the United States can be planted upon the North Pole itself if the proper support be given to those who have the patience and determination to attempt and pursue the indicated plan.

When the Arctic regions shall have thus been made known and the necessary scientific observations secured, then the attention of explorers might be directed to the South Pole, and under a corresponding system that vast and unknown Antarctic region will yield up its secrets, and man will at last "have dominion over all the earth," and prove his obedience by attempting to "subdue it."

Very respectfully and sincerely yours,

R. W. D. BRYAN.

To Capt. H. W. HOWGATE, U. S. A., *Washington, D. C.*

(From Captain George E. Tyson, of the *Polaris*.)

WASHINGTON, D. C.

Captain H. W. Howgate:

DEAR SIR: I was very agreeably surprised to see your letter, published some time ago in the New York papers, containing a proposition to Congress to appropriate money, ship and the necessary equipment for another expedition to endeavor to reach the North Pole, and I heartily concur with you in the plan therein suggested as the most practicable yet devised. It is a matter of no little surprise to me that there has not been more of an outpouring of American enthusiasm toward the achievement of the success of this great enterprise, and that, too, when we consider the magnitude and great importance of the work. It is unquestionably a noble effort, and the scientific societies of the country would do well to unite in memorializing Congress relative thereto. Now is the time, and if this Government fails this year, through a spirit of parsimonious economy, to appropriate the means necessary to the furtherance of this project, England or Germany will, in all probability, secure the honor of this great achievement.

GEORGE E. TYSON.

(From Captain H. C. Chester of the Polaris Expedition)

To the Editor of the New York Times:

Having had some experience in Arctic exploration, and being familiar with its dangers and difficulties, my attention has been called to the letter of Captain Henry W. Howgate, published in the "Times" on the 26th of December, I beg to express my thorough approval of the plan submitted by Captain Howgate, as I believe it to be the only way by means of which the Pole can be reached. All future explorations tending to solve the mysteries of this extreme northern region will have to be prosecuted by means of gradual advances made from some main depot. Exactly the same idea was entertained by Captain Hall. When we were at the furthest point of land, about 82° 8′′, in October, 1871, we looked at the so-called impenetrable sea of ice. Then it was moving ice and water. From its smoothness we felt very sure that when the colder weather set in we would have but little trouble traversing the channel in the spring. We should have endeavored to have crossed Robeson's Straits, and would have tried to gain a point of land visible northwest of us, which land we called Cape Union, and which we calculated was some sixty miles distant. If Captain Howgate's suggestions of establishing a party at or about Robeson's Channel, or to the west of it, is ever carried out, I think these people would by progressive stages reach in time the much desired goal. As to the obstructions mentioned by Captain Nares, all I can state is that such impediments did not exist in my time. The reasons why I suppose they cannot be so formidable are founded in the following observations: When in May and June of 1872 we lay with the boats and crew of the *Polaris*, twenty-five miles from the ship, on the floe ice, waiting for an opening in Robeson's Channel, in order to cross it, during four weeks' time the straits were blocked with ice, but this ice was all moving south. We found no opening for a month, and were unable to use our boats. This ice went southerly at the uniform rate of about one and a half miles an hour, and was never checked, save when the winds blew south or southwest. If, then, the strait was filled with ice moving southerly, such an impassable barrier of ice as Captain Nares speaks of must have been found at a point very much further north than the land designated by us as being Cape Union. I do not think there could have been much of an error as to the distance we supposed ourselves to be from this Cape Union, and the North Pole could not have been more than 420 miles north of it.

When Captain Hall and the writer undertook the fourteen day sledge journey, when we worked our way along in the twilight, Captain Hall said to me, "I am satisfied that the only way to reach the Pole will be for us to carry our provisions across Robeson's Channel, to form a depot on the other side, and from thence take out parties. It is work we must lay out for ourselves this spring." I believe, had Captain Hall lived, he would have carried forward the work just as Captain Howgate proposes that is, by establishing depots and making progressive stages. Captain Hall's untimely death, on the 8th of November, 1871, prevented his accomplishing this design. I think in order to prosecute the plan proposed by Captain Howgate, there would be no difficulty in procuring thirty men accustomed to Arctic travel, who would ultimately achieve success. As to fresh blood food, I am positive that, at least in the neighborhood of Robeson's Channel, the musk ox can be found from May to October. I shot the first musk ox on the Polaris plane in 81° 40″ during the latter part of September. With the crew of the *Polaris* in the latitude of 82° we killed twenty-four musk oxen. I do not believe there would be any trouble in provisioning thirty men yearly with this fresh food. I therefore must freely indorse Captain Howgate's views, and say with him, "Let an expedition be organized to start in the spring of 1877, and I firmly believe that in 1880 the geography of the Polar circle would be definitely settled, and that without loss of life."

H. C. CHESTER.
PHILADELPHIA, *Saturday, December* 30, 1876.

(From Mr. Robert Seyboth, a member of Dr. Hayes' expedition.)

Captain H. W. Howgate:

* * * * * * * *

I have not the slightest doubt if a sufficient number of energetic men, well selected and officered, can acclimate themselves to the terrible severity of Arctic winters, the greatest difficulty in the way of the discovery of the Pole will have been overcome, for such a party and depot could be used as a base of operation from which to push forward, in favorable junctures of temperature and their accompanying condition, successive posts, each one to be permanently held until the next was established, and until some favoring season made the open Polar Sea a navigable reality.

The great question to be answered in considering your scheme is the possibility of sustaining human life at such high latitudes for a sufficient length of time. I do not hesitate to answer this question in the affirmative. My own experience during a stay of nearly two years within the Arctic circle, and with an expedition that possessed none of the comforts and safeguards usually provided for Arctic explorers, warrant me to believe that a systematically conducted plan of colonization, such as you propose, would meet no insurmountable difficulties in the effort to sustain life and sufficient robustness to carry out the work of exploration. Scurvy, the great enemy of former explorers, can be entirely avoided by adopting the proper hygienic precautions, as has been fully proved by the late Captain Hall, who spent several years in succession in company of the Esquimaux, in perfect health and without assistance from the outside world.

It is a noteworthy fact that American whalers, who frequently remain two or more successive winters in the Arctic regions, do not suffer from scurvy while wintering, but are almost invariably afflicted with the fell disease during the homeward voyage. Why? Because they do not hesitate to eat plentifully of seal, walrus, bear and even whale meat, all of which is readily obtainable in the highest latitudes. To this diet I myself found no difficulty in becoming accustomed, and, consequently, did not suffer from scurvy until after the enforced resumption of "salt junk" on the homeward stretch. Granting, then, the possibility of colonization, I fully believe that the adoption of your scheme would strike at the root of former failures in Arctic explorations, for it substitutes the steady conquest, step by step, in place of the spasmodic and unsustained efforts hitherto made at the sacrifice of untold treasure and the loss of great and noble lives.

Very respectfully,   ROBERT SEYBOTH.

(Action of the Milwaukee Chamber of Commerce.)

CHAMBER OF COMMERCE, MILWAUKEE, *January* 13, 1877.

Whereas this Chamber has been and is now interested in matters of scientific interest, and has by its action largely aided and forwarded the inception and perfecting of the present Signal Service of the United States, as applied to commerce and navigation ;

And whereas this Chamber is desirous of expressing its interests in and good will toward all measures calculated to forward and extend scientific explorations and experiments which may have even an indirect bearing upon such subject; therefore,

Be it resolved, That we cordially approve of the proposed appropriation of $50,000 by the General Government to aid in the establishment of a temporary colony, for the purpose of exploration and scientific research, at or near the eighty first degree of north latitude, under the direction of the President of the United States and with the advice and counsel of the National Academy of Science, to carry into effect such detailed observations in the sciences of meteorology, botany, geology and climatology, together with the perfecting of the geography of unknown regions extending to the North Pole, as may increase the sum of human knowledge, redound to the credit of the United States and sustain the reputation and honor of our country already won through the labors of De Haven, Kane, Hayes, Hall and other eminent explorers in the northern Polar Seas.

Resolved, That the Secretary be instructed to transmit to our Senators and Representatives in Congress a copy of the foregoing preamble and resolutions, and to respectfully request their careful consideration of the same.

The foregoing preamble and resolutions were introduced at a meeting of the Chamber of Commerce of Milwaukee, January 13, 1877, and unanimously adopted.

[SEAL.]   N. VANKIRK, *President.*

W. J. LANGSON, *Secretary.*

[Introduced in House of Representatives January 20, 1877, and referred to Committee on Appropriations.

Introduced in Senate January 26, 1877, and referred to Committee on Appropriations.]

(Action of Indianapolis Board of Trade.)

BOARD OF TRADE, INDIANAPOLIS, *Jvnuary* 23, 1877.

Whereas there is now pending before Congress a bill introduced by General Hunter, of Indiana, appopriating the sum of $50,000 to aid in the establishment of a temporary colony for the purpose of exploration and scientific research at some point near the eighty-first degree of north latitude, under the direction of the President of the United States, and to carry into effect such detailed observations in the sciences, together with the perfecting of the geography of unknown regions extending to the North Pole as may increase the sum of human knowledge and redound to the honor of our country; therefore be it

Resolved, That this Board of Trade favors the passage of the bill, and that the Secretary transmit to our Senators and Representatives in Congress a copy of these proceedings.